A CAPFUL OF WHISKY IMPROVES THE PORRIDGE

SHELDON CLAY

outskirts press

Table of Contents

Foreword

After a couple of decades at an advertising agency writing print and tv ads, I was curious about what I could say if I had more than 30 seconds or 325 characters. I started writing essays. Observations. Reflections. The occasional opinion. Here are 14, covering a little more than five years. If there's a theme here, it's language. The pictures language can paint. The moments it can capture, and translate into something larger. The way language becomes a sort of scenic overlook for the life going on around us. Enjoy the view.

Frozen in Our Tracks

March 1st. Zero degrees Fahrenheit. The high temperature for the day. Same as the day before. And for who knows how many days before that. I've lost count. As the infamous Polar Vortex has taught us all too well this year, air temperature is only part of the equation. On this particular day the wind chill adds another 21 degrees of negativity to the mix.

I look out the window and the world is buried under a heavy blanket of snow. The sky is the color of dull metal. Below it everything is still. This is different from the Christmas Eve "all is calm" sort of still. It's a fretful, shivering quiet. We huddle inside, full of worry over frozen pipes and smashed bumpers and whatever else the long winter may yet have in store for us. A glacier-sized slab of ice slid off my roof the other day and crushed the gas grill.

March 1st, the whole world feels frozen in its tracks. Not the sudden, immobilizing fright that normally implies. But a slow, numbing, soul-crushing kind of motionlessness as the cold pushes its way deeper and deeper into the wheels of everything.

The streets of Minneapolis are narrow canyons surrounded by high walls of banked snow. The pavement has vanished under a thick layer of ice. It looks like the kind of dirty ice scientists describe as the stuff that makes up meteors. The ice you get in the absolute zero of deep space. Average speed on the city streets hovers around 20 mph. Using your brakes at a stop sign is a cruel joke, sending the car twisting slowly sideways toward the center of the intersection.

Read the financial press and you see how deeply the cold has reached into the nation's bones. No one has gone to the mall the first two months of the year. No one has the gumption to buy anything. Economic indicators have turned as negative as the wind chill.

Even here in the hardy north our commuter rail line has gone from its stellar 96% on-time record to a makeshift plan using city buses to pick up the passengers that get stranded for hours on frigid platforms every time a switch freezes or a stalled freight train blocks traffic. We're literally frozen in our tracks.

My father, a railroad man, would have understood. He knew railroads make their money on a good fall harvest, and need to husband that money to keep the trains running when the winter turns hard. He once showed me a photo of a giant locomotive buried by a blizzard on the North Dakota plains. He died exactly five years ago, on March 1st.

That was a less frigid March. The great recession was just plumbing its depths and no one yet knew how the whole thing would end up. The feeling of trying to climb out of some endlessly deep glacial crevasse was still ahead of us. That day I took a break from the sadness and the funeral arrangements and went cross-country skiing on the thawing snowpack. It's something I'd done so often with my dad when he was alive. I could feel his presence as my skis glided ahead. My father was not a man to let things drift into motionlessness. He knew how to make the trains run on time and how to make the wheels of government turn the way they ought. Like so many of his generation. Now they're leaving the stage and maybe that's why our first truly hard winter in years feels even harder.

March 1ˢᵗ, five years later. Even the skiing is devoid of forward motion. No one has been on the trails for days. The incessant winds have blown over the tracks, and hardened the snow. Its surface is so cold it tugs at my skis instead of letting the wax glide. Its depths pull my poles in so deep the grips end up by my knees, giving me a hunched-over gait. Picture Quasimodo trying to cross-country ski.

The frozen weather mirrors the way the whole world has been going. The Ukrainians protesting in the Kiev Maidan lit a flickering candle of hope. It was immediately blown out by the icy breath howling down from Vladimir Putin's Russia. In our own country the buoyant optimism of Barack Obama's election ran headlong into the self-righteous anger of the Tea Party. The bitter winds blowing back and forth across the aisles of Congress haven't let up since. This winter has been creeping into our bones for longer than we know.

The way it all feels was captured perfectly by C. S. Lewis in *The Lion, The Witch and the Wardrobe.* "It's always winter, but never Christmas." For Lewis, unending cold was a metaphor for loss of faith. That may be a big part of the icy grip we're in now. Loss of faith in ourselves. In our government. And yes, in our spiritual lives. Eventually faith returns to Lewis' ice-gripped Narnia, and with it the thaw. My favorite part of the story is how Lewis describes the way the thaw starts with just a glimmer, a green blade of grass, a warm breeze. Then starts gathering steam until it becomes unstoppable. I think he's borrowing from the biblical parable of the mustard seed. Just a little has a powerful effect.

That's something to think about, especially for those who've made a trade out of pedaling bitterness and an absolute zero brand of negativity in recent years. I'm thinking politicians in particular may find this a good time to keep a finger in the wind, just in case it starts start blowing warmer.

Absent another ice age, the thaw will come. At least meteorologically. When it does the spirits held down so long will rise. Like spring floods, once they start rising they may just keep going. The reversal of a truly harsh winter is something we haven't experienced in some time. Who knows how far the feeling of things coming unfrozen might carry us. Or what debris might be swept away by a sudden upsurge of optimism. We can only hope. That's why in Minnesota we love the seasonal extremes not just for how they change the landscape. But for how they change us.

March 5, 2014

The Walls in My Life

There is a small wall at the back of the yard where I live. It once served to divide the lot and contain the dog.

Then the dog learned to jump the wall. It didn't take long for us to tire of chasing him through the neighborhood, so we added a higher fence. Now the dog exhausts only himself as he runs around the yard. But there is an unintended consequence. We see less of our excellent neighbors across the heightened fence.

There are two sides, it seems, to every wall. In Robert Frost's poem *The Mending Wall,* the neighbor thinks it wisdom to constantly re-stack the stones that nature has tumbled down and repeat the phrase, "Good fences make good neighbors." The sage poet is not so easily convinced.

"Something there is that doesn't love a wall," he writes. "That wants it down."

As a writer my early instinct was to surround myself with walls. The theory was that being alone with my thoughts would improve them. For a time I had the last office at the end of a long rat warren of hallway.

If I buried myself deeply enough in a project I could escape notice for days on end.

I was upended when the ad agency I work for moved to a building with a flashy new open-concept design. There was nary a wall in sight. It meant the end of writing as I knew it. So you can imagine my surprise when instead of dwindling to nothing the flow of ideas improved. Collaboration came without effort. Bringing down the walls made me a better writer than I ever was alone.

A giant wall between the United States and Mexico is the most concrete symbol to rise out of the *commedia dell'arte* that is our 2016 political season. "I would build a great wall, and nobody builds walls better than me, believe me," Donald Trump said in the speech announcing his run for the presidency. He says that his wall continues to be the best applause line at his strange campaign rallies.

Trump himself likes to compare his idea to the Great Wall of China. That took an entire millennium to build and some historians estimate the work killed as many as 400,000 peasants. But as Trump likes to point out, "They didn't have Caterpillar tractors."

Even so, if we decide to enclose our nation we should opt for something with the scale and anachronistic battlements of China's Great Wall. Thousands of tourists visit it every day to marvel at the architectural wonder and snap a selfie. There isn't much a wall can do to shore up our border — the top smugglers all use tunnels these days — so thinking of it as a tourist attraction might at least give the project some small utility. Trump wants the Mexican government to pay for everything. But if we're going to make the wall fun for tourists I'd suggest outsourcing it to Disney instead. They'd know how to build something that mimics The Great Wall of China, and might even run a monorail along the top for sightseers.

Given the way government projects usually work these days, the more likely scenario would be something on the order of the grim Berlin wall. That was erected quickly and on the cheap, built mostly of concrete slabs, razor wire and gun emplacements. You can get an idea of how such a wall might function by watching the scene from the movie *Bridge of Spies* where Tom Hanks is riding the train back from East Berlin and stares out his window as guards machine gun a group of young people trying to escape over the wall to freedom.

This might all be fun for Trump's people to think about, but in truth I don't believe he has any intention of building a wall. Trump is a real estate developer by trade. The first thing developers do when they have an idea for a new project is get a big glossy piece of artwork to sell the concept. Picture something with white gleaming crenellations airbrushed against a sapphire sky, and maybe a 36-hole championship golf course in the foreground on the U.S. side. I've been to Trump's website. Nowhere is there an architectural rendering to inspire the Trump legions to start quarrying stone or baking adobe or whatever it is they have in mind that might actually become a wall across our southern border.

No, the wall is a symbol. Its careless use by the Trump campaign is destined to become yet another disappointment for the hard-pressed middle-class voters who might think he has something real to offer. The Trump ascendency has a lot of smart people scratching their heads, but it's not complicated. Trump exists because politics, like nature, abhors a vacuum. And absolute zero is exactly what the party he now leads created when they decided to spend the entirety of the Obama presidency working to deny him any accomplishment. By thinking they could ring-fence an entire presidency the Republican Party has managed to spend eight years depriving both themselves and the nation of oxygen. Even now they refuse to consider a Supreme Court nominee that most of them agree would be wonderful, just to name one glaring example.

They walled themselves in like some ill-fated character from an Edgar Allen Poe story. And into the void left behind seeped the noxious gas of Trump's rhetoric. The thing about walls is they're built by those who've lost faith in the power of their ideas, and have no option left but to retreat behind a physical barrier. The border fence. Transgender bathroom laws. Climate change denial. Voter suppression. It's all walls.

I don't think any of the big political players quite appreciate the remarkable irony of the wall as a political symbol. The Republican Party reached its high point of the past century when Ronald Reagan stood in Berlin and shouted, "Mr. Gorbachev, tear down this wall!" It's reached its low point as Donald Trump sits in his tower contemplating a new one.

May 5, 2016

The Slates

There is something in us that wants to sail. Even though a sailboat might seem like an anachronism in an age when air travel has made going anywhere you want more a thing to be measured by inconvenience than adventure. Then again, maybe that's reason enough.

The opportunity for me came in an email from a friend. He quoted Herman Melville: "Whenever I find myself growing grim about the mouth; whenever it is a damp, drizzly November in my soul; whenever I find myself involuntarily pausing before coffin warehouses, and bringing up the rear of every funeral I meet; and especially whenever my hypos get such an upper hand of me, that it requires a strong moral principle to prevent me from deliberately stepping into the street, and methodically knocking people's hats off – then, I account it high time to get to sea as soon as I can."

My friend had a line on chartering a sturdy 40-foot sloop named the Frodo. He proposed that a group of us set sail for the Slate Islands in the far northern reaches of Lake Superior.

There are people who can tie eight different kinds of knots and tell you the name of every line descending from the rigging of a sailboat.

They'll take you deep into the art of sailing. I am not one of those people. My perspective is that of one used to keeping both feet on dry land. This would be only my second time venturing onto the wild waters of Lake Superior.

The Frodo was a good boat to do it in. The boat was built in Finland, with a wide beam and deep, heavy keel to hold her own on the Baltic Sea. She's not new, built in the early 1980s. But she has an authentic teak deck and nicely polished appointments in the cabins. Me, I'll take a weathered deck as a good sign that the boat and body of water are well enough acquainted to remain on friendly terms throughout my voyage.

Five of us motored out of Thunder Bay at precisely 8:27 a.m. on Day One, hoping to cover half of the roughly 100 miles to the Slate Islands on our first leg. The high cliffs on the Canadian shore are remote and rugged, and I never got tired of watching the scenery drift by. The wind had yet to make an appearance. The Frodo's big diesel chugged away, making a steady 5.2 knots.

Running the motor is not the highlight of a sailing adventure. It feels like you're on a tractor plowing water. So it was grins all around when the wind finally stirred off our starboard bow. We made ready to sail.

Even in relatively light winds the process of raising the sail on a big boat gets the pulse going. You turn straight into the wind, and for a few heartbeats all is chaos. There's a lot of physics going on. The sails snap in the wind. The boom fights to break loose. Then one last tug on the halyard brings the sail to the top of the Frodo's tall mast. It seems like it takes longer than it actually does. Then it's time to fall away from the wind and regain control of the boat. We unfurl the genoa – the oversized jib sail attached to the front of the mast – and feel the strong pull as the sails take the Frodo forward.

That's the moment, each time you experience it, that you understand exactly what's so good about sailing. The artificial rumble of the motor is gone. The ropes creak as they tighten against the power of the wind. Seven knots. Then seven-point-four. Wind, waves and boat connect like a single living thing, and riding at the center of it all is you.

Day Two showed us the wilder side of the world's biggest freshwater lake. First came an icy wind blowing off the deep, frigid expanse of water, straight toward our bow. The rest of the country was experiencing a massive July heat wave, but I came on deck dressed for November. Wool socks, thermal shirt, a heavy polar fleece, wind- and waterproof shell, and a knit hat up top. Wearing everything I had in my duffel felt about right.

This was our crossing day. An 86° compass heading would take us straight over the big water to the Slate Islands. The wind shifted just enough to make a close-hauled sail possible. This is the point of sail where the mainsail and genoa are set tight to the boat. If you get it right the sails mimic the aerodynamics of an airplane wing, pulling the boat forward into the wind. If you get it wrong and point the bow too directly into the wind you're "in the irons." The sails luff uselessly and the rudder loses all power to steer. Bill, the most experienced sailor of our group of friends, did a fair amount of eyeballing and fine-tuning. Then declared the sails set.

Being on deck in big water when the wind starts blowing is a thrill ride. The wind speed often hit 25 knots, and the Frodo dipped her bow under some waves. If being on top was exhilarating, going below was another experience entirely. It's like stepping inside a cement mixer. Your internal gyroscope goes haywire. There are handholds everywhere, and you need them as you get tossed about by the pitching cabin. All of us came away with a few bumps and bruises from the rough crossing. Perhaps more alarming, Bill, the aforementioned experienced sailor and our captain for the voyage, ended up leaning over the side and sending his breakfast to Davy Jones' Locker.

As if the winds and waves weren't enough, the Frodo hit a bank of fog just short of the islands. We kept a wary eye on both the water ahead and the big compass positioned near the wheel. Just as it began to feel seriously creepy seeing nothing but gray in every direction, two points of land emerged out of the fog. They marked the entrance to the large interior bay of the Slate Islands. Somehow, we'd managed to keep the Frodo straight on course through everything Superior had thrown at us.

Day Three dawned with the water mirror-smooth. We spent the next two nights anchored in McGreevy Harbor, deep in the interior of the Slates. Then a third night just around the southeastern tip of the arpeggio in a rocky bay named Patterson Harbor. The surrounding days we had free to explore the Slate Islands. I've never seen anything quite like them. Rugged sea cliffs preside over pristine bays and inlets. There is a large herd of woodland caribou. We managed to spot just one, but it made for a majestic sight as it picked its way along a secluded cove.

The most striking feature of the Slate Islands is their remoteness. By any normal means of conveyance, you are quite simply a long ways from anywhere. The sum total of our encounters with humanity is as follows. Two men working at a lighthouse. A young couple camped on an island. A delightful 86-year-old woman who makes a habit of visiting the Slate Islands every year in her pretty white yacht. A small group of researchers studying the caribou. There can't be too many other places left on Earth where you have such a vast and stunning natural treasure virtually to yourself.

Wednesday we began making our way back towards the Canadian mainland. The winds were directly to our stern, which is not an easy point of sail. Even a slight shift in the wind can cause the boom to jibe unpredictably and knock an unwary sailor over the side. We rigged a spar to hold the head sail out to port, and a boom preventer to hold the mainsail safely out to starboard, and sailed wing-and-wing to our next anchorage at Woodbine Harbor. According to the notes penciled on the Frodo's charts, Woodbine is a favorite of previous visitors. That opinion was seconded by The Bonnie. That's what we called the thick spiral-bound book that guided our comings and goings. The book's real name is *The Superior Way*, written by a longtime sailor named Bonnie Dahl, who spent decades cruising Lake Superior and discovering its secrets. The Bonnie was our bible for finding the best anchorages and threading our way through the teeth of the rocks that guard them. Woodbine Harbor proved to be as gorgeous as promised. Once there we picked up a fresh cargo of biting flies and mosquitoes, which I spent the night in my berth battling with a rolled-up magazine.

On a sailboat you are either looking for wind, or dealing with too much of it. That makes sailing a perfect metaphor for life, which rarely comes at a person in even measures. Solid little philosophical nuggets like this come easily on a sailing voyage. In some part this is due to the unique level of focus you have on a sailboat. It's just dangerous enough that the mind is always engaged. The other part is that humanity has been at it for so long. As one of our group put it, "What I love about a boat is that everything has a purpose and a lot of them go back hundreds of years. People have gotten this figured out for us."

In a sense, what we were doing wasn't that different from what Henry Thoreau did when he set off to live in his cabin on Walden Pond. It was a voyage of self-reliance and spiritual discovery. Like Thoreau we were living deliberately, with only the supplies we carried with us. Although, in full disclosure, our stock of wine and good whiskey well-exceeded Thoreau's theory of living simply. And there is this difference: if you're not paying attention, Lake Superior will kill you a lot more quickly than Walden Pond.

We got the full spectrum of wind conditions on our last full day of sailing, from the moment we weighed anchor in Woodbine Harbor. The day began with alternating bands of bright sunshine with zero wind, then thick fog with zero visibility. One long blast on the foghorn followed by two short ones is the proper signal for a boat making way under sail.

By late morning the fog lifted for good and the wind began to blow hard, straight at our bow. No sailboat can make headway directly into the wind, so the answer is to tack. That means sailing at an angle to the direction you actually want to travel. We'd set a tacking course that would take us some five miles out into the open water, then come about and tack back towards the coast. Progress is made in a series of giant zigs and zags.

The wind hit fifteen knots and we put the first reef into the mainsail. A reef folds the sail down toward the boom to reduce its size and power, like going from a V-8 to a six-cylinder engine in your car. We put the second reef in at twenty. Then the wind hit twenty-five knots and we reefed in the genoa as far as it would go. After that all we could do was hang on, unless we wanted to find a sheltered cove to wait out the blow. That thought probably occurred to a few of us the final time we came about near the safety of the coast and began another tack back out toward the wild open water.

The waves came at the Frodo like a range of small mountains, and I scrambled for pills to calm the tempest rising in my stomach. I'm not sure which one worked. But luckily it didn't take long before something did. The lesson learned on such a day is a simple one. Trust the boat. The Frodo had been across the Atlantic. She's outfitted for racing. It's liberating to replace the silent scream trying to grow in your brain with the idea that this is what the Frodo was built for. Then hang on and enjoy the ride.

A day hence from our wild lurch into Superior's 25-knot headwind we would be re-entering a world with its own unsettling turbulence. We'd left behind the mixed-up summer of 2016 and its end-of-the-world vibe. It would all be waiting for us when we came back. But sailing brings you back different. The useful thing it taught me is that perhaps what a democratic society like ours really does is tack, just like we were doing out on the lake. People can't head straight into all the terrifying dislocation coming at them right now. So they point themselves out toward the deep, uncharted, crazy waters. Then, hopefully, come about and head back toward the coast before they lose sight of it entirely. In the age of sailing you needed a strategy to get where you wanted to go. Most often it involved setting a course that veered in some unexpected opposite direction. That gave people a sort of wisdom we would all find useful today.

But before I had to worry about any of that, nature had one last phenomenon to show us. Lake Superior acts like a giant refrigerator, and for the past week this had kept an icy wind blowing across our bow. But as we approached our destination we came around a point and suddenly were sailing into wind that had been blowing across the mainland with its withering heat wave. It was the same 20-knot wind, but in the space of about a minute it went from beer cooler to blast furnace. One of our group has spent his career managing wildlife preserves. Even he was astonished at the magnitude of what Mother Nature had just pulled off.

Along with the strange hot wind blowing out of Thunder Bay came my first cellphone signal in a while, and it was time to start noticing the things missed during eight days off the grid. I missed 527 emails. I missed the entirety of the Republican convention, for which I shall be eternally grateful to the good ship Frodo. I missed my afternoon coffee, although we did on occasion adhere to the British Royal Navy tradition of a full-gill ration of rum for the crew (served with a wedge of lime to ward off scurvy). I missed running, but not so much. Standing on the heaving deck of a sailboat requires constant small adjustments to keep your feet braced. It's like a day-long session doing the core muscle maneuvers you get taught in a Pilates class. I missed hot showers. The evening routine was a quick jump off the back of the Frodo into the fifty-degree water of Lake Superior. Followed by an even quicker scramble up the ladder to stand on deck and try to suck the air back into your lungs.

I missed the soft touch of my wife, and a weekend visit by a newly mobile and endlessly curious toddler named Oscar. Other than these last two important items, there is little that I missed as much as I enjoyed heading into the wind and the waves on a compass point less traveled.

August 3 2016

CARDU COUNTRY HOUSE
KNOCKANDO, ABELOUR, SCOTLAND
+44 1340 810895

A Capful of Whisky Improves the Porridge

It's an old chestnut that travel brings wisdom, but who are we to argue? Recently I found myself on a plane back from Scotland with my head filled with ideas like some old philosopher, scrambling for a pen to write it all down. Here are the field notes from the trip.

In the month of May, Scotland glows yellow. There are daffodils everywhere growing wild and planted in vast gardens. Daffodils were originally brought to the British Isles by the Romans. Long after the Empire's old walls and roads crumbled the daffodils remain to astonish us.

Raise your eyes a little higher on the landscape and the theme continues. A scrappy shrub named common broom is in full bloom, painting the hillsides golden yellow. How the entire countryside managed to be color-coordinated throughout my trip was a delightful mystery.

The thing about getting out into the middle of a country not your own is you get to take people at face value. It's a welcome escape from the conversations at home, where the available subject matter is so often trapped in the narrow tribalisms of work or politics or, worse, dipped from the shallow pool of what was seen on the morning TV news. The talk between people thrown together by travel is about things that matter. The strange abundance of pheasants running across the country lane between Knockando and Craigellachie, for example. Or the possibilities malted whisky brings to cooking. Scotland has its own arguments I'm sure, especially as I was visiting in the weeks just prior to the United Kingdom's vote to depart the European Union. The beauty of being the one wandering through is you don't get pulled under by the rivers of poison that spew out of such a debate. Distance from home is an elixir for enjoyable conversation.

The castles dotting the Scottish countryside stand as a testament to civilization's long withdrawal from the wandering life. We may be roamers at heart and on vacation, but in practice we mark our boundaries with stones and retreat behind battlements to fiercely defend them. Tour a Scottish castle and you see this process displayed like the concentric rings of a tree. You are quite literally dissecting history.

The oldest part of the castle is the medieval tower that stands at the center. These are tall, narrow structures and they made up the entirety of the living space during the years when William Wallace and Robert the Bruce fought their wars with the English. The old towers were cold and claustrophobic, full of murder holes to shoot arrows or pour boiling oil through, and steep, easy-to-defend staircases.

Spreading out from the central tower are the more comfortable sections built as castles got bigger under the three turbulent centuries of rule by the Stuart kings. The great lords were getting more powerful, and needed space to house the men-at-arms they put to work defending their interests.

Finally came the defeat of Bonnie Prince Charlie in 1746, which marked the end of neighbor battling neighbor in Scotland. The idea of your home being a castle passed into metaphor. The great lords and ladies cut windows through the thick walls and covered over the rough stone with plaster. The old fortresses became fine country estates surrounded by sprawling formal gardens.

Once they quit fighting the English and each other these same Highlanders would form some of the most storied regiments defending the far-flung British Empire. The castles on the tourist route are full of museums and memorials commemorating their exploits. Even more compelling were the words I found carved into a single headstone in a quiet cemetery near the inn where I was staying. Buried there are a man and wife who died during the reign of Queen Victoria, both at the ripe old age of 77. Reading further down the stone you come to the sons of the family. A lieutenant of the Second Scottish Horse, killed in 1901 in the South African Transval, aged 23 years. A lieutenant of the 6th Seaforth Highlanders who died in 1917 at Aubigny-En-Artois, aged 24 years. A captain killed in 1918 at Shiraz, Persia, aged 29 years. There was no interpretive plaque. What more could there be to say?

Traveling through Scotland, it feels like you rarely take a step that hasn't already been trod at some point in the past. Stroll down a sidewalk and there's a grassy spot marked by three tall stones left behind by a long-vanished tribe of Picts. Look at the side of a building and there's an inscription telling you Bonnie Prince Charlie passed this way on the long march to his final battle at Culloden. I took a nature hike along a rushing stream. Even there, deep into the forest, I came across an ancient stone bridge. Just enough to remind me I was sharing the trail with history.

Some might use such ever-present reminders of things past as an excuse to spend their days looking backward. But the Scottish are a breakfast people. Tucking in to a full-whack Scottish breakfast is a sign of faith in the day ahead. That may explain why the people of Scotland so overwhelmingly and optimistically voted against leaving the European

Union, even if their side ultimately lost to the crowd determined to turn its back on the future.

As a meal, breakfast has been in decline of late. Who has the time anymore? There's even a new university study that questions the traditional role of breakfast as the most important meal of the day. The breakfast skeptics have obviously never begun their day in the dining room of the Cardhu Country House in Knockando. There are kippers on the menu, and a traditional Scottish breakfast built around a delightful herb-flavored haggis from the butcher in nearby Aberlour. Americans consider eating haggis a brave act, as it is banned by our FDA. I found it delicious as long as one doesn't inquire too deeply into its makings.

But for me the thing was the porridge. Here were ingredients worth inquiring about. Porridge is what Americans less poetically call oatmeal, ladled into a bowl with a swirl of honey and a pour of the thick local cream. But the best part the good proprietor of the Cardhu Country House saved for last, smiling his helpful smile as he revealed it. "A capful of whisky improves the porridge."

And there it was. The secret to starting the day with an epic bowl of porridge. Maybe the secret to a lot of things. Find pleasure in the unexpected places, and the unorthodox combinations. Don't let the relentless goad of the news ticker steal your life. Be ever mindful that we are given gifts like travel, love and the taste of good whisky, and most days that is enough. Or as the proprietor of the Cardhu Country house put it, a capful of whisky improves the porridge. Rarely does a philosophy for living get articulated with such profound simplicity.

Sept 6, 2016

Christmas Morn

Oscar, who is not yet two, is already asleep. He was awake by 5:30, and danced his way through the ribbons and tissue paper and torn wrapping all morning. Until enough was enough and down he went for an early nap.

My beautiful daughter woke up this morning feeling gloriously well, which for me was Christmas gift enough. She'd been ill on Christmas Eve and sprinted for the bathroom to throw up as Mass began. Her quick recovery may be minuscule in the pantheon of Christmas miracles, but I'll take it.

The even greater gift she gave me this morning was a note, accompanied by a small watercolor. "I can't wait to see what 2017 brings for you," she wrote. This to a father who's been losing sleep nightly worrying about what manner of horrific 2017 we might be handing young people like her. There are so many people of bad intent in high places right now. Men, mostly, who've learned that fear and division are the easy path to power and are working mightily to turn the world away from peace and goodness. But then here is hope. Born in the optimistic words of a girl to her father.

Also among the gifts this Christmas was a small figurine of Mary, Undoer of Knots, wrapped and put under the tree by my Jesuit brother-in-law. It's unusual, so different from the Mary of the Christmas carols watching over her child as he lays sleeping in the manger. This image of Mary working to undo the knots of discord and anguish and despair we tie our lives into is a favorite of Pope Francis, I was told. Pope Francis is himself spreading a sort of populism in the world. But his is not the harsh populism that has so upended the year just finishing. It's about healing, not hurting. With all that's going on in the world right now it offers a reassuring counterbalance.

So just now I'll be satisfied with the optimism of my daughter and the bright humanity symbolized by a humble Pope and his devotion to Mary, Undoer of Knots. These are reminders enough that there are still forces of good in the world and they stand against the smug tide of bitterness that has overwhelmed the headlines and cable news of late. We are not yet in a post-truth age. Powerful truths abide and today we celebrate one of them.

It is eleven o'clock on Christmas morning and Oscar, who is not yet two, is already asleep. There is such peace in a small child asleep. In this, I find profound hope.

Dec 25, 2016

The American Regency

With apologies to Mrs. Pence, consider this unlikely scenario. The vice president has been secretly watching *Game of Thrones* on his laptop. He sees himself as the character Littlefinger.

I know, this is a guy who is uncomfortable meeting female co-workers without his wife present. The idea of him watching *Game of Thrones* is a stretch. But the Internet is a serpent constantly dangling its temptations before the upright, so let's go with it.

Mike Pence begins to think of himself as Littlefinger, at least in his role of lord protector and master behind-the-throne manipulator if not in his role as owner of the palace brothel. Then the vice president wakes up one morning with an idea to save the republic.

Mike Pence's big idea is this: turn the Trump presidency into a regency. If you're heading to Wikipedia to find out what the hell is a regency, I'll save you the trouble. It's when the legitimate ruler happens to be an infant, so an advisor or group of advisors is appointed regent to make sure there's an actual adult running things.

The only country with an active regency right now is Liechtenstein. Raise your hand if you even knew there still was a Liechtenstein.

It's an old concept, and maybe better suited to a monarchy than a democracy. But consider this. Every analysis we read about why the Trump administration has gone so haywire comes down to the same thing. We basically have a second grader trying to govern the most powerful nation on Earth. Throughout most of western political tradition the remedy for that very situation has been to set up a regency.

I'm pretty sure there's nothing authorizing this in the Constitution. But the real thing we need to wonder about here is the president's constitution. Both its unfitness for the job of governing, and, even more, its inability to handle something like removal from office. There are rumblings about Impeachment in the press. Or even more intriguing, removal under the 25th Amendment. The latter is a process few have even heard about that allows the vice president and a majority of the cabinet to come together and decide the president is "unable to discharge the powers and duties of his office," and vote to replace him. But can you imagine? Trump would leave the nation a smoldering cinder before he'd let some "so-called" constitutional process steal his power.

So Mike Pence sees how Littlefinger quietly manipulates the levers of power in *Game of Thrones* by naming himself lord protector of the boy ruler of The Vale, and comes up with his plan for The Regency. He sells it as a way to avoid the destructive fight any attempt at actually removing the president from office would bring down on the country.

Pence cuts a win-win deal with Senate Majority Leader Mitch McConnell and Minority Leader Chuck Schumer. The three decide to put the big political fights on ice for four years and form The Regency to quietly keep the government functioning. Chuck Schumer gets to keep some semblance of American government intact. Mitch

McConnell gets a way to keep his party from being sucked down a Trumpian black hole. Mike Pence gets to spend four years hatching plots just like Littlefinger. By mutual agreement Paul Ryan and Nancy Pelosi are left out of the arrangement. Fixing the dystopian House of Representatives can wait until after the 2020 Census.

You may ask why Donald Trump would go along with such a plan. But think about it. By all accounts he hates how hard this whole being president thing has turned out. The Regency off-loads the hard part onto people who actually have some interest in doing it. The role of the president becomes something more like the figurehead role Queen Elizabeth II plays in England's parliamentary democracy. Trump might actually be good at this.

He still gets to parade around the White House and sign things he doesn't understand, surrounded by big grinning crowds. He still gets two scoops of ice cream at state dinners while everyone else gets one. He's no longer frustrated by constant White House leaks, since everyone involved has a vested interest in keeping The Regency on the QT. Most important, the president remains in charge of the remote control for the big 60" flat screen he had installed in the White House.

The president has mostly done a good job meeting one-on-one with other heads of state, and that continues under The Regency. It makes for some nice travel opportunities and weekends at Mar-a-Lago.

Plus, the president will be able to continue the important work of documenting his inaugural crowd size and photocopying his electoral maps. This will keep him occupied while The Regency handles the more mundane chore of running the country.

Decades from now The American Regency will be remembered as a relatively stable period when people of reasonable intent were able to put aside their differences and come together to heal a divided nation. Like so many petulant second graders, the president will be gotten onto the right meds to help him be less disruptive. He'll actually achieve some popularity as the harmless mascot of a sort of good-natured Americanism. The furniture we currently think of as Mid-Century Modern will come to be called Regency Period. It will be more popular than ever.

May 24, 2017

Being Two at the Zoo

I was brought to the zoo by my grandson the other day.

He's at that happy age between two and three, where the assignment is to absorb every ounce of information from his surroundings. He focused his powers of concentration on that.

I took care of the more mundane tasks associated with our visit. Getting us there in a car. Handling affairs at the zoo's admissions desk.

I also pushed the stroller. When my grandson noted something of interest the drill was as follows: squat down, lift him from the stroller, hold him up so he could see to the back of the habitat, set him back in, and repeat. The Marines could use this exercise at boot camp

It was a cool, rainy fall Friday. Other than those groups that had arrived on the school busses lined up at the back of the parking lot, most children of prime zoo-going age were away tending to the more bookish side of their educations. If you got the rhythm of your visit right you could avoid the big school groups and have the place virtually to yourself.

We were at Minnesota's new zoo, it being built just over 40 years ago. The other zoo in the Twin Cities is the Como Zoo, built in Victorian times.

There is a lot to like about the Como Zoo, including its urban setting and an adjoining glass conservatory that takes its design cues from the old Crystal Palace in London.

But on this rainy fall Friday it was the new zoo. Its defining characteristic is space. The zoo's director once told me the other zoo directors envy his ability to create big natural exhibits for the animals to lose themselves in.

What fascinates me about a zoo with so much space is you never know what to expect. The star attraction of one visit may be a total no-show the next time you're there, sleeping behind a tree somewhere at the far back of its habitat.

I'm sure the animals like this better and so do I. There's something right about never quite knowing what you'll encounter. It's like a trip into the wild. The random element, luck, always plays a role.

The random elements are even more at play when you see the zoo through the eyes of a two-year-old. You arrive with a well-defined plan of attack. But your tiny captain determines the line of march, calling out preferences from his seat in the stroller.

This adds a magical quality to the trip, in particular if you're a grandparent grown accustomed to traveling with the adult herd and its straight-ahead proclivities. Right now you're two years old yourself, hunkered down at the toddler perspective, your eyes as wide as his. The boundaries separating you from the wild fade away, and there you are. In it with the animal.

The penguins pop one at a time out of a cave at the back of their enclosure. Comedians taking the stage at The Improv.

The Komodo dragon, from the perspective of a two-year-old, is every bit the real dragon from the storybooks. He's climbed up high in his lair, looking at you with ancient, steely eyes. He pokes at the air with a forked tongue as long as your forearm. You are transfixed by his stare, unable to move on.

And then, another wonder. Down a long tunnel, you find yourself before a massive glass wall. On the other side is the tropical reef exhibit. It teams with bright marine life in dizzying motion. And right in the middle of it all, a guy. A diver, blowing a stream of bubbles up to the surface of the water, methodically cleaning the coral.

To an adult this is routine maintenance done on a quiet fall Friday at the zoo.

To the two-year-old it's breaking the fourth wall of the imagination. The guy! What is he doing in there? What's on his feet? What is that thing he's holding?

If that diver can be in there, surrounded by so much wild and exotic life, so could any of us. On the drive home my grandson talks only about the guy. I'm going to be that guy when I grow up. I'm going to be that guy for Halloween.

I take this as a good sign. The animals you meet at the zoo are on the job. Working animals employed as ambassadors for their endangered species and vanishing wild. We adults can read the plaque about the threats of ocean acidification, increased carbon dioxide in the air, water pollution and careless tourism. When you're not yet three years old it's enough just to make a connection with the fascinating animals.

Hopefully you will grow up into the sort of person that wants to be on their side.

For my grandson, seeing himself as the guy in the diver's suit working in the middle of all that astonishing life made the connection even stronger.

It was dark the next morning when he woke up. The sun wouldn't rise for well over an hour. What do you think that guy is doing, he asked me. I imagined the guy was still sleeping.

I rested my head on the edge of the bed and asked him if he didn't think he might want to sleep a little longer. No, he smiled, full of energy. He composed a small morning song to get things moving:

> *Hold me down from the bed, Papa.*
> *Hold me down from the bed.*
> *Rum tum tiddly tum,*
> *Papa, hold me down from the bed.*

A mash-up of roots music and Winnie the Pooh. Obviously there would be no more sleeping. I lifted him out of the bed. We went downstairs in our pajamas to make breakfast and talk about the guy swimming in the tropical reef exhibit at the zoo.

November 11, 2017

Martin and Francis

Lutherans are not given to noisy celebration, so you might have missed this. The Lutheran Reformation turned 500 years old on October 31. That was the day in 1517 when Martin Luther nailed his famous Ninety-Five Theses questioning the pope's authority to the door of the Castle Church in Wittenberg.

Those who assign a more hands-on role to the divine might say it started a dozen years earlier. In 1505 a bolt of lightning knocked the young wannabe lawyer off his horse, convincing him to switch his career aspirations from law to religion and forever blowing the idea of a monolithic church into pieces. The first shot of the revolution, fired by God.

That's the way the history was taught me, a kid in Sunday school sitting on a metal folding chair in the church basement. Luther's ideas changed history, but what I remember from Sunday school is the lightning strike. The bright revelatory flash winning out over more nuanced theological discussion.

I've been reading up on Luther during this 500th anniversary of his revolution. He was a popular teacher and wrote all the time, using

Gutenberg's newfangled printing press to spread his pamphlets around the countryside. This earned him a crowd of followers and made it difficult for the church to burn him at the stake, as was its usual remedy for his sort of troublemaker. Otherwise the whole thing might have been over in a hurry.

Lutheranism caught on across Germany and Europe, Protestants and Catholics spent the next century trying to murder one another, then The Enlightenment arrived and religion was finally eased out of the governing equation. Now we all live together in a world Martin Luther would find astonishing.

He would be especially surprised to learn that right now the guy who's talking a lot like he did is the current pope. The Antichrist himself, as Luther liked to describe his old adversary.

To further stand history on its head, the opposite role once occupied by the corrupt Catholic hierarchy currently goes to the leaders of Protestantism's own evangelical movement.

A role reversal for the ages.

When Pope Francis looks at the culture war conundrums thrown his way and says, "Who am I to judge," he's echoing the central argument Luther made all those years ago. "My conscience is captive to the word of God," Luther said before the tribunal, steadfastly refusing the right of anyone other than The Almighty to pass judgment on our sins.

This is confusing to some, who don't like ambiguity when it comes to questions like sex and marriage. They prefer their orthodoxy handed down straight from the high places. Uncut. Unfiltered. Dot the i's. Cross the t's. Don't leave room for waffling. New York Times Columnist Ross Douthat, who writes with a fine conservative voice, complains "the only Catholic certainty now is uncertainty."

And so it is, but that's not the pope's doing. We live in uncertain times. 500 years ago it was a world swinging from Medieval to Modernity, pausing to admire some Renaissance art along the way. Today it's a world running on warp speed every hour of the day. The spiritual remedy for this amount of disruption isn't a judge. It's a shepherd. Francis knows that. So did Martin Luther before him.

In Luther's day the fight was over the sale of indulgences. You mortgaged the house to buy a slip of paper. When your time came it was supposed to give you a free pass out of Purgatory and straight on through the pearly gates. They went like hotcakes.

But dig a little deeper into the can of worms Luther opened up with his Ninety-Five Theses and it's the same story we're dealing with in the current political moment. You find churchmen hopelessly caught up in a lust for worldly power. The indulgence business was really a big confidence scheme cooked up between the pope and a German prince with his eye on high political office. This unholy alliance was supposed to fund construction of the pope's grand new basilica in Rome and get the prince appointed Archbishop in Mainz, which sounds like an ecclesiastical job but was really the most powerful political position in the land.

You see how quickly things get complicated when the church worships the false idols of greed and power.

This is the hard truth evangelical voters face today. They've thrown in their lot with politicians who make a cruel joke out of everything their faith stands for, and they thought the result would be worth it. Heaven on earth, with the entire Republican Party singing like a choir of angels. Instead, they get what? Judicial appointments? The devil delights in such transactions.

And so the evangelical flock has been led astray and there's no one to show them the way back. Only the wolves are happy. In Alabama, State Auditor Jim Zeigler defends the schoolgirl-chasing ways of his party's Bible-thumping Senate candidate Roy Moore by pointing out that Mary the Mother of Jesus was a teenager, and Joseph so much older. The entertainment business calls this jumping the shark – the moment it's painfully obvious the show has gone on too long.

We are all human and flawed. Sooner or later the temptations of worldly power will get the better of those who anoint themselves as the upholders of all that is true and good. The moralizing judges end up on the wrong side of history. It's the shepherds we remember.

November 21, 2017

Travels with Chuck

It's hot already this July morning. The sky is an unblemished sapphire. I'm running one of the longer of my usual neighborhood routes. A last burst of activity before the long road trip ahead.

The plan is for my son and I to drive his car across North Dakota and Montana, over the high pass in Glacier National Park, and on to his new home in Portland, Oregon.

The car is in what you might call its declining years. We'd convinced ourselves this was the practical way to get it moved out to the West Coast, along with assorted houseplants and a couple of bicycles my son didn't want packed in the moving van. In reality, it was my opportunity to go road-tripping with the son who was about to move with his sweet young family half a continent away from our home state of Minnesota.

The car is a 2001 Acura 2-door with leather seats the size of Lay-Z-Boys. My grandson has christened it Oldie Goldie Dentmobile. This is the same three-year-old who has informed us his name is Bless You Banana.

My son simply calls the car Chuck, because both the car and the name originally belonged to my late father. I guess the car is a sort of patrimony. My son still keeps my dad's old cane in the trunk.

The Advil hasn't kicked in yet as I hit the halfway point on my morning run. I feel as old and full of kinks as the car itself. I hope both of us make it all the way to Portland.

The first leg of the trip is up Interstate 94 to Bismarck. One giant farm blends into the next. Most of the interesting towns are somewhere off the highway, identified only by the water towers peering over the tree line.

Night One, Bismarck ND. Our hotel is on the high ground north of town and we can see huge thunderheads spread out across the plains. They ring the city, fired by the setting sun. We stand in the parking lot watching the light show until fat rain drops start plopping all around us. By the time we get up to our room the rain is coming in sheets. The wind drives it straight through the seal in the hotel window.

The next morning we cross the Missouri River, and The West begins. It's as abrupt as switching on an old Gary Cooper movie. We're driving through rolling rangeland populated mostly by nothing.

We pass a sign telling us we've crossed into the Mountain Time Zone, so we gain an hour. We put the extra time to good use: a hike in Theodore Roosevelt National Park. Since the idea is to walk not drive, we grab the first trail leading off the road into the park's south unit. After a half-mile the trail dead-ends into the Little Missouri River. Apparently the trail's "difficult" rating includes wading the river to reach the path continuing up the opposite bank and into spectacular badlands. There's no telling how deep the muddy water might be.

We walk the other direction instead, up a grassy trail to a prairie dog town, and pick up a load of wood ticks. All afternoon through Montana we're pulling them off our arms and legs and tossing them out the car windows.

Northern Montana is even emptier than North Dakota. The rolling hills turn to big, grassy buttes. Chuck was originally equipped with a premium sound system and it still works, although patching in an iPod is a challenge. We dial up a batch of Bob Dylan studio sessions from the mid-sixties. He is even better in these raw, unproduced versions. His harmonica sounds as lonely as the highway ahead. The car rides smooth as long as we don't push things too far past 80. Everything is perfect.

Then a rhythmic thump starts coming from the front end.

It doesn't go away. So we pull over to investigate. The thump comes from a little box under the dash by the passenger's left knee. The iPhones have been blinking in and out of "no service" for a while, but right now there's a signal. My son searches the Internet while I check the oil. The culprit is a little electric motor that's supposed to operate the ventilation system. The car will run without AC even if its passengers might not.

Our route takes us across Highway 2 toward Glacier. The old road is the northernmost highway in the U.S., originally built in 1919 to link a series of muddy auto trails and connect Portland, Maine to Portland Oregon. When we come to a crossroads the arrow pointing to the right simply says "Canada."

White crosses dot the shoulders of the highway, marking spots where people have died in car crashes. There are an alarming number of them considering how unpopulated the surrounding countryside is. On some stretches it seems like a mile doesn't go by without a white cross. Sometimes they come in pairs. On one curve in the road nine crosses sit atop a single post. Seeing them is a little like seeing the endless rows of white markers in a veterans cemetery, each one a silent testimony to a story we'll never know.

That night, in Shelby, Montana we sit at the bar in a restaurant-slash-casino. Everything along this stretch of road is a something-slash-casino. Gas station. Motel lobby. Pizza place. Laundromat. Picture a low building with a few slot machines and a huge neon sign and you get the idea. For some reason they've taken the shotgun approach to casinos rather than having one glitzy establishment where you might walk in and imagine yourself as James Bond in a tuxedo playing Baccarat. This is unhelpful when what you're really after is a decent meal.

After bar food and a couple of beers we come up with a plan. Chuck has already shed one part. Who knows what might go out next. So we decide to skip the high pass on the Going-To-The-Sun Road and take the easier road around the southern end of Glacier.

We call this The Conservative Plan and toast it with our beers. It will hopefully get us over the mountains intact, and as an added bonus make more time available for a hike in the western end of the park. The southern route is less famous, but also less traveled. It turns out to be stunningly beautiful.

At one point I see "TRUMP" spray-painted in 10-foot letters on a rocky cliff, a strange act of desecration so far from the boiling pot of Washington. But we're driving through Glacier Park on the 4th of July. It's hard to think anything other than magnanimous thoughts. The president is scheduled to travel to Montana the following day, but only as far as Great Falls. I wonder what might happen if he could somehow be loaded into one of his golf carts and taken up into these mountains. Imagine a man whose entire world consists of glass towers, manicured golf courses and flat TV screens come fact-to-face with the actual power and beauty of creation. Maybe it would help.

There is a good trail right inside the western entrance to the park, but it includes the possibility of a bear. A woman at the trailhead parking lot tells us she'd turned back when she saw a mother grizzly and cub. Since a number of paths branch out from the trailhead we figure there's a decent chance we'd be headed down a bear-free one. For good measure we decide to talk loud while we walk, just to make sure we don't surprise any bears coming around a bend.

Talking nonstop with your son for a couple of hours while walking on a trail filled with wild flowers and ringed by breathtaking mountains makes for one of the top moments in a father's life.

We talked about his new home in Portland. We talked about the one he is leaving behind in Minnesota. My wife and I are going to miss having he and his family close-by and there's sadness in that. But sharing the excitement of your kid's next adventure is also part of parenting, even if that means sharing it from afar.

That excitement kept bubbling to the surface as I walked and talked with my son. I can be content with that.

The days ahead would bring the serious work of unpacking. Managing the huge piles of packing paper the movers had wrapped around anything even remotely breakable. Bringing the new house's window hardware up to the standards of someone accustomed to Minnesota winters. Arranging the toys in my grandson's bedroom so it feels like home when he arrives. Arranging my daughter-in-law's spice drawer in the kitchen, for the same reason. Until you've done it, you could never imagine just how connected you feel to someone when you're unpacking their household item by item.

But the unpacking still lay down the road, as would an easier life for Chuck. The car was headed for a neighborhood where it's easy to walk or bike to just about everything. It would be spending most of its days blissfully parked in the garage.

We still had one important stop remaining before we left Highway 2 to merge onto a final stretch of interstate. Troy, Montana. My dad was born in Troy, and spent the first five years of his life there. Then the town got clobbered by the Great Depression and the family headed back to the Midwest.

But my dad never forgot Troy. He always talked about getting back there. I felt an almost mystical connection to Troy as we drove through, even if I've only been there a couple of times in my life. It's still one of the prettiest places on earth, with green tree-covered mountains rising above the wild Kootenai River. My grandson is not that far removed from the age my dad was when he left Montana. I wonder if he'll feel the same sort of connection to Minnesota. His move is taking him half a continent away from the relationship we've enjoyed. That doesn't feel so forbidding now that I'm covering the entire span one mile at a time.

We can solve for distance.

It's time that most often comes between us and the people we love. We let the busy little things eat our lives. Before anyone realizes it whole hunks of lifetime have slipped away, and we're scrambling to catch up.

I learned this on a road trip that came into being because my son refused to let go of an old car. The miles that separate us also connect us. Chuck will be living the easy life in a tuck-under garage. I'm more determined than ever to make sure the path away from my garage stays well worn.

July 25, 2018

The Roomer

Lars was a fixture at family gatherings when I was a kid. I come from a big, extended family of Scandinavian descent, so I always assumed he was a great uncle once-removed or something like that.

It was only recently that I learned he was in fact a roomer who'd once lived in the front bedroom of my great grandmother's house.

Lars was the oldest person I knew, or at least it seemed that way. There was a timeless quality to him. Where others might bring a Jell-O mold or plate of cookies to a family gathering, his idea of a hostess gift was more along the lines of a pick-up truck load of newly split firewood.

He was a Norwegian bachelor farmer straight out of one of Garrison Keillor's old Lake Woebegone stories, living alone in the Northwoods of Wisconsin and spending his free time chopping wood. The two things he had in abundance were free time and available trees.

He didn't have any family. At some point I imagine he adopted ours. Back in the 1920s Lars was a one of a succession of young men who got off the boat from Norway and landed in my great grandmother's front bedroom for a few weeks or months while establishing themselves in Minnesota and the surrounding environs.

My great grandmother was born Eline Ronning in Norway, and that's as much as anyone knows about her early life. She was raised by her grandparents. When she turned 18 she left Norway for the New World. She never spoke again about her childhood, except to say she remembered the Norwegian countryside as beautiful.

She married a streetcar conductor in Minneapolis. When he died early from a heart attack she was left with four kids and her house in the Northeast neighborhood now famous for its wealth of microbreweries. She made ends meet by sewing dresses at home and renting out the front bedroom. Nowadays we'd call that the Gig Economy and the Sharing Economy. She was doing it a hundred years before they became a thing.

In today's Sharing Economy you can go to to a site like Airbnb and find a slick algorithm working to connect millions of hosts and guests. I can't tell you how the same basic process worked in the first decades of the last century, but somehow it did. A young man coming over from Norway knew he could find a safe place to land and get his feet under him in my great grandmother's house.

As my mother put it, "It was a small world between Norway and Northeast Minneapolis in those days."

Most of the young bachelors from Norway followed the example of Lars and fanned out into the surrounding countryside to work small farms.

The final Norwegian to occupy the front bedroom was a man named Hoken. He decided he liked the city better than the idea of finding himself a farm, and made the rooming arrangement permanent. Even during the years when my great grandmother rented out the whole rest of the house and lived with her kids in North Dakota and Wisconsin, Hoken kept the front bedroom.

He was still there in the 1930s when my grandfather moved the family back to Minneapolis and bought the house from his mother-in-law. My mother remembers Hoken as a distinguished man with white hair who walked with a cane. He had a stately demeanor and kept mostly to himself. He took his meals out every day. Everyone called him Hoke.

Hoke had the front bedroom. What my mother cannot remember is how my grandparents found space for everyone else. They had six kids. My great grandmother continued to live with them well into her nineties. It was the Great Depression. Then the war. People made do.

My daughter has spent much of the past year living in Airbnb rooms a month at a time as she travels around the country, completing her fourth year of medical school. Currently she's in New York City, occupying one room of a two-bedroom apartment owned by a single mother with a 7-year-old daughter.

Past is prologue, as they say. Or, as the Book of Ecclesiastes puts it:

> *What has been will be again,*
> *what has been done will be done again;*
> *there is nothing new under the sun.*

A lot of the same economic undercurrents that once brought Norwegian immigrants to my great grandmother's house in Minneapolis have now brought my daughter to her room in the Bronx. Too many people looking for not enough housing. Not enough money in the paycheck to make ends meet. An available room becomes a sort of currency.

Everyone is fascinated by the way the web and its algorithms are fueling the current sharing economy. I'll be more interested in seeing how the human side of the equation plays out. How will sharing a home with strangers change the way we think about family? At a time when social media are making our connections less human, will this push them in the other direction?

Thanks to my great grandmother taking in roomers I gained a relative whose sinewy tenacity I admired. My dad always said Lars could work rings around us younger guys, and I took that to heart. When I'm his age, whatever that age really was, I hope someone would think to say that about me.

Feb 5, 2019

Still Motorcycling

The evening has turned surprisingly cool for this late in June. Even with my motorcycle jacket zipped to the chin, the night air is slowly making off with whatever core body heat I had remaining.

I'm riding around the southeastern shore of Lake Minnetonka, headed in the general direction of the bright lights of Minneapolis.

Beyond that I have zero idea where I am.

This is as it should be on a motorcycle. A wise friend once wrote getting on a motorcycle is seeing the country at ground level. You're mixed in with the scenery in ways that, for most people, disappeared when the saddle horse went out of style.

If you're not getting a little lost you're not doing it right.

I follow the taillight of the guy in front of me, a friend who's lived much of his life out by the big meandering lake and knows the roads. Behind me is the headlight of another friend.

We stick to a tight formation.

Even when we run through a patch of construction, where the loose gravel wobbles the wheels nervously, I keep a constant vigil on the tail-light in front of me. I check and the headlight behind me is steady in my mirrors.

We've ridden motorcycles together for 40 years, been friends even longer.

Feels like it was yesterday.

Our lives had spun off in directions as different as the motorcycles we were riding. None of that mattered.

Something about our friendship got solidified by the passage of time. It reminds me of the way minerals seep into the bones of some ancient Pliocene sea creature and create rock.

The friendship was right there waiting to be rediscovered — just as good as it always was — when one of us sent a random text. "Let's go for a ride this summer."

This particular June Wednesday is just past the summer solstice and the days are at their longest. The sun is still hot in the sky as we grab a beer at a local hangout named Bunny's, then head west of the city to explore the small towns and Main Streets that dot the shores of Lake Minnetonka and beyond.

Our machinery is as eclectic as our personalities. The engineer and inventor in the group rides a new-aged techno scooter, with a stealthy fast 800 cc engine and tiny electric motors that raise the windshield and tuck in the mirrors. My most adrenaline-fueled friend rides a fiery red Honda street racer from the 90s. The one of us who always seemed to have something or the other old and British arrives on a beautifully restored 1950 Ariel Square Four. That's the bike that attracts all the admiring glances when we pull into the pretty town of Victoria to wander among the vintage roadsters and muscle cars lining the streets for their regular Wednesday Classic Car Night. For me, with my romantic era take on most things in this world, it's a centennial edition Harley Low Rider.

There is not a lot of opportunity for conversation when you're riding with a group on motorcycles. Maybe a few shouted words at the occasional stoplight. The small towns and cafes are where we finally get the chance to do some catching up. One of the things we marvel at is how a friendship that started before middle school could become something enduring.

Motorcycling can't explain it all, but it's a solid metaphor for the things that cement a bond. There's a shared danger, and that's certainly part of it. You share bigger things as well. Freedom. Discovery. A sense of awe at being a part of the countryside you're riding through.

These are things the passing years don't wear away.

We spend a few hours melting away decades. Then the sun drops over the horizon, and we feel the warmth of the evening chasing after it. The old Ariel isn't rigged for safe nighttime riding. The vintage taillight is the size of a thimble. The Lucas electric system in old British bikes is famous for winking out at inopportune moments. So it's long past time to fire up the motorcycles and make our way back to the real world.

There's one last shouted conversation at a stoplight before I split off onto the freeway toward home.

"Lot of bugs out tonight."

And so there were. I'd been getting pelted the last few miles, like standing in front of a low-intensity sandblaster with the occasional thunk from something the size of a shelled peanut. I make a note to clean up before climbing into bed. Experience has taught me waking up to a pillow full of bug parts is no way to endear oneself to one's wife.

The final stretch home. Chrome parts glitter in the lights of the instruments. I feel the pull of the big Harley, aimed toward whatever life has in store for me next.

Things that endure have become so rare in this world. Maybe that's the reason some of us still ride motorcycles.

July 13, 2019

How George Floyd Changes Us

What makes George Floyd different?

That's a question worth asking right now. The unrest in the streets has become more peaceful but just as insistent. The news has moved on to the next police killing of an unarmed Black man. But the question remains.

Why, of all the horrific scenes of Black Americans killed by law enforcement, did it take a 46-year-old security guard dying under the knee of a Minneapolis cop to finally blow the lid off an unjust system?

The answer will give us a clue to just how big a possibility for historic change we're looking at this time around.

The Reverend Al Sharpton turned to the Book of Ecclesiastes in his eulogy for George Floyd. "To every season there's a time and a purpose." The time has come, the reverend thundered.

Former Secretary of State Condoleezza Rice echoed that in a piece for the Washington Post. So often the outrage fades before anything can change, she wrote. "But something tells me — not this time."

I think we all feel that.

The same dreadful story has come at us again and again. The killings of Ahmaud Arbery and Breonna Taylor were still fresh in the news on the day of George Floyd's fatal encounter with systemic racism. The fuse was not far from the powder keg.

Then there is the brute inhumanity of this particular death. At the close of his eulogy Reverend Sharpton asked everyone to stand in silence for an interminable eight minutes and forty-six seconds, marking the time George Floyd spent dying. It brought home the icy depths of the cruelty involved.

But there is something more at work here. I'm a storyteller by trade, so I look at how it fits in the larger story of America. George Floyd has become the Everyman in an American tragedy.

It's one thing to howl with rage at the terrible injustice experienced by some distant other person. An Everyman character takes the "other" out of the equation. The injustice becomes real. Internal. Even for those of us whose life has been a relative cakewalk.

Everyman — or Everywoman — is a literary device that shows you the story through the eyes of someone you can identify with. Its power comes from making you feel part of the story. Mr. Smith Goes to Washington. The terrified kid puking in his landing craft in an old WWII movie. The women who found the voice to say #MeToo.

It's ironic, because during his life George Floyd would have had a hard time finding himself pictured as the Everyman character in much of what we see coming out of the entertainment industry. That's just part of what needs fixing right now.

But the Everyman that makes a story powerful isn't necessarily the one that looks just like you. It's the one that reveals something about you. That's what makes George Floyd the man for this moment of history.

So many of our shared fears came together in the last eight minutes and forty-six seconds of George Floyd's life. "I can't breathe," at a time when the coronavirus kills by robbing us of oxygen. Deeply entrenched racial injustice, at a time when the pandemic has struck so disproportionately in communities of color.

A lawless cop, at a time when a lawless president is deliberately working to asphyxiate our democracy. I don't think it's lost on anyone that the brutal way Trump's military treated protestors in the nation's capital may be just an omen of what's to come as we get closer to the November election.

In an earlier turbulent era a folk singer from Minnesota wrote, "You don't need a weatherman to know which way the wind blows." Now the death of an Everyman figure in Minnesota has brought us face-to-face with the consequences of injustice left too long to fester in our society.

An interesting thing has been happening in public opinion polls. After so many years of the nation being split straight down the middle, there are signs of us easing back together. Roughly two-thirds of Americans support an overly careful re-opening of the country from the long coronavirus lockdown, despite the severe economic pain involved. And now similar numbers support those protesting the death of George Floyd, even though the first few days of civil unrest were frightening to many.

This is back-of-the-envelope social science, but I think it's a number to watch. Two thirds of us sticking with something, even when it's hard. That hasn't happened in a long while.

You feel that sense of solidarity when you visit the site of George Floyd's death. The blocks around 38th and Chicago in Minneapolis have become a shrine. Strewn with flowers. Covered with street art.

There's a solemnity to the place. The kind you might experience walking an old battlefield like Gettysburg. Only this isn't about history. You're standing at the epicenter of something new.

George Floyd died because America's original sin has never stopped haunting us. Perhaps it's no coincidence that in another time and another place the cross also killed by asphyxiation. The nation is in sore need of redemption.

Momentum for that has been building — especially through the perseverance of the Black Lives Matter movement. Now a terrible convergence of events has burned a face and a name into our collective consciousness. The outpouring of grief and outrage is shared by a broad swath of humanity. That's how a narrative gains the power to change history.

This old storyteller doesn't see George Floyd letting go of us any time soon.

June 20, 2020

Do You Wear a Mask in Your Dreams?

I had a dream where I was wearing a face mask. This was a first for me.

I don't remember much of the dream. Just the fragment about the mask. I was at a charity function. The sort that used to be held in some nondescript hotel ballroom, back before everything turned into a Zoom call. I sat at a chair pulled away from the table, socially distanced I imagine, watching a presentation at the front of the room.

When I turned toward the rest of the people at my table they looked at me in horror. A black cloth mask was dangling uselessly from the arm of my chair. I put it on.

Everyone breathed easier.

I keep hearing that people have been dreaming weird since the start of the COVID-19 pandemic. There's so much to process by the end of a day. Some nights my dreams exhaust me.

Scientists tell us dreams are an artifact of the brain sifting through the day's events. Sorting, consolidating, storing what's important in long-term memory.

So there's significance to my dream. Wearing a face mask has now worked its way deep into my subconscious.

I was an early adopter of masks, at least compared to most here in the U.S. My son insisted on it. He's a critical care and pulmonary specialist in Portland, Oregon.

It was late winter. He was working brutal shifts as Covid cases surged in the Pacific Northwest. Hooking patients up to ventilators. Sometimes having to shout through all the protective gear he was wearing to make himself heard during end-of-life conversations. When we talked on the phone I could hear it in his voice. Those end-of-life conversations haunted him.

At the time the official guidance from the CDC still did not recommend masks for the general population. My son told me that wasn't evidence-based, it was resource-based. Why tell everyone to wear masks if there were none to go around? I should definitely be wearing a mask, he said.

I was as self-conscious as anyone steeped in America's tough-guy culture the first time I tied on the sole paper surgical mask in my possession. Only the anonymity of knowing people probably wouldn't be able to recognize me anyway made it better. In the months since I've accumulated an odd assortment of masks for my occasional trips into the world.

Masks themselves have become the most insane symbol of America's pathologically bipolar response to the pandemic.

I don't need Freud to explain what was going through my head the night the mask came into my dreams. It was sadness.

I was hunkered down in the pretty Southeastern Minnesota tourist town where I spend much of my time. On a nice summer weekend the town almost feels normal, and that's the problem. From my little nineteenth-century brick house up on the hill it's easy to see the care-free crowds milling about the center of town.

Families spilling out of minivans. Teenagers from the surrounding countryside spilling out of the beds of pickup trucks. Big groups pedaling down the bike trail that cuts through town. The patios of the town's two bars were crowded and loud.

In normal times I would have been happy for all the local merchants, some of them good friends. In a tourist town in Minnesota you only have a few warm months to make your livelihood.

Now, in our time of contagion, it makes me sad. Too many people crowded together. Not enough masks. Maybe there are no random superspreaders lurking among the crowds this weekend. Maybe the nice weather that mostly kept people outside added a sufficient buffer of safety. No one really knows. There's a Russian Roulette quality to the whole thing.

It's a microcosm of all that's gone wrong with the response to the pandemic in the U.S. I watch the crowds enjoying a sunny afternoon and know the schools probably won't open the way everyone had hoped this fall. The town's wonderful professional theater will stay dark through the season. I worry my son will again be having way too many end-of-life conversations. Our laissez-faire approach to battling the pandemic has condemned us to this grinding twilight where no one is safe and nothing is normal, even if people desperately wish it to be so.

So is it time to give up on any hope for the old spirit of collective can-do that's seen the nation through its worst moments? Maybe not. I've been reading *The Splendid and the Vile*, Erik Larson's new book about Churchill in the early months of World War II. It chronicles his long, often exasperating campaign to stir Roosevelt and the U.S. into action. This country has always tended to get where it needs to be by a long and torturous route.

There is an unfortunate lack of hard science about how, or even if, wearing a mask protects you on an individual level from the novel coronavirus. Most of the studies are about wearing masks in the aggregate. The societies that do a good job of wearing masks tend to do much better against the pandemic. My theory is wearing masks is a part of getting a lot of other things right as well. Most importantly the idea that we're all in this together. Having some respect for the science. And for our fellow citizens.

So I'm encouraged if masks are starting to work their way deeper into our subconscious. It might be a symbol of something bigger on the horizon. I was just on a Zoom call for work, and a colleague said she'd realized she's been wearing a face mask in her dreams.

August 9, 2020

Lilacs

The lilacs are blooming in the far corner of the yard, so I brought some to my mother.

This is a yearly tradition for me. I used to bring them on my birthday in early May. But climate change has left the typical Minnesota spring cooler than it used to be, and tall shade trees have crowded closer to the lilacs. Now the delicate purple blossoms arrive too late for my birthday.

When they do their corner of the backyard is filled with fragrance, and so is my mother's kitchen.

She has often told me the day I was born my father brought lilacs to her room in the hospital. The young couple had just moved into a house with a yard and a garden, the kind of idyllic mid-century setting that gave birth to the sprawling baby boom generation. He didn't want her to miss the sweetness of lilacs in full bloom.

I was the first of their children to live long enough to come home from the hospital. So the lilacs took on a bigger meaning – a kind of charm for both my mother and myself. The whole hospital celebrated my good health, she told me recently over a glass of wine. This was an enlargement of the birth story I'd been hearing all my life.

I knew I had two older brothers who'd died in infancy, within days of their birth. There's a genetic snafu lodged in the family tree. If the chromosomes get lined up the wrong way it can prove fatal to male babies.

I confess I'd never really thought that deeply about the details. It all happened before my time. But here were my parents making their third trip to the maternity ward. The hospital staff would have been aware of, some of them intimately involved in, the unfathomable sadness of the two previous visits. So of course there would have been a lot of people holding their breath. Hoping the third time would prove the charm.

"You were perfect," my mother told me over that glass of wine. For the sake of humility let's not take that in the general sense, but as a particular reference to the lack of any fatal imperfection in my genes. The picture I had in my head when I heard about the hospital staff celebrating is the happy one we've seen on the TV news this past year, when Covid patients make a miracle comeback after months on a ventilator and doctors and nurses line the hallway to cheer as they leave the hospital.

My kids, miracles in their own way and now working in the medical profession, have been a part of such celebrations. "Nothing is new under the sun," the old psalmist said. Maybe he was referring to this sort of past-to-future connection.

Life changes in a heartbeat, and that's why it's so precious. One moment you're worried about getting the crib assembled in the nursery. The next you find yourself in need of a tiny coffin.

I never knew where my two older brothers were buried until a few years ago. My mother and I made the trip to the part of Wisconsin where she and my father grew up. It took us a few rounds of, "turn here, no, wait, now turn there." But we found the small-town cemetery. Then the grave of my dad's mother, who died while he was in high school. My young parents, faced with the unexpected need to bury one new-born, and then another, found some small comfort in laying them in the existing grave alongside the mother who left this earth years before the rest of us became a family.

I was born into a mix of tragedy and joy.

I wonder if that's always been an undercurrent in my life, nudging me along. I think occasionally of the early courage of my parents and I'm filled with admiration. And somewhere down inside, a prodding obligation to be useful.

We all have undercurrents in our lives. Family histories. Traditions born of joy and sorrow. Things we may be only vaguely aware of, yet push us to become who we are. I think we're all feeling their tug a little more strongly right now as the world struggles to put the fears and social isolation of the pandemic behind us.

The public health authorities tell us the vaccine is proof against the virus and all its variants, at least so far. Me, I keep eyeing the trusty N-95 mask hanging on its peg by the door every time I go out. It's been my suit of armor through so much. The idea of walking into a crowd without it feels like stepping off the lip of a volcano.

I read about the uneven vaccination rates around the country, and the way sensible public health guidelines keep getting stirred into the boiling cauldron of politics, and wonder if the best course might be to just find oneself a cave and become a proper hermit.

Instead, I think of the opening lines to T.S. Eliot's long poem *The Wasteland*. They were written as Europe was trying to climb back from the twin disasters of the First World War and the horrific Spanish flu.

> *April is the cruellest month, breeding*
> *Lilacs out of the dead land, mixing*
> *Memory and desire, stirring*
> *Dull roots with spring rain.*

So we're back to lilacs. They're sturdy, unobtrusive plants that spend much of the year quietly lining our yards and streets, until prodded by Mr. Eliot's spring rain to emerge in a brief yearly riot of scent and color.

Look lilacs up on the Internet and you learn they can live 100 years. The span of time between that early global pandemic and the one currently plaguing us. A century ago the neighborhood I live in was famous for lilacs. It's perched on the main highway west of Minneapolis, which in the spring blushed pink and purple with so many blooming lilacs it was called Lilac Way. The name is gone but many of the lilacs remain. They've witnessed a lot.

Last year the lilac blossoms in my backyard stayed on the branch until they finally withered and fell to the ground. The first terrifying surge of coronavirus infections was giving way to a second. No one was bringing cut flowers anywhere. We were living strangely outside of time, adrift from such rites of spring as bringing in a bunch of delicate purple flowers to adorn the kitchen table.

Lilacs as I've described them here are a cyclical phenomenon. They mark time the way it was understood by the old agrarian societies, making their annual contribution and never asking for much in return. I've rarely had to tend to mine with the hose or pruning shears. Lilacs would be a good symbol for those who hope that the pandemic is indeed receding, and they will be deposited back into "normal" as they've always understood it.

But time stopped flowing in that sort of reliable cycle long ago. The seasonal rituals that once anchored humanity's concept of time have mostly faded away as well. Something deeper always whispers us forward.

Large-scale change is coming for society as we depart the strange chrysalis of the global pandemic. There is little in the pages of history to give assurance that it will be for the better. But I've been listening to those deeper whispers this past year. Feeling the undercurrents. They give me hope it will be.

July 26, 2021

CPSIA information can be obtained
at www.ICGtesting.com
Printed in the USA
BVHW071413061221
623342BV00006B/58